POETRY FOR CHILDREN

The Little Land

By Robert Louis Stevenson
Illustrated by Rebecca Thornburgh

Harrison County
Public Library

The Child's World

Distributed by The Child's World®
1980 Lookout Drive • Mankato, MN 56003-1705
800-599-READ • www.childsworld.com

Acknowledgments
The Child's World®: Mary Berendes, Publishing Director
The Design Lab: Kathleen Petelinsek, Design

Copyright © 2012 by the Peterson Publishing Company. All rights reserved.
No part of this book may be reproduced or utilized in any form
or by any means without written permission from the publisher.

Library of Congress Cataloging-in-Publication Data
Stevenson, Robert Louis, 1850–1894.
  The little land / by Robert Louis Stevenson ; illustrated by Rebecca Thornburgh.
    p. cm.
  ISBN 978-1-60973-153-3 (library reinforced : alk. paper)
  I. Thornburgh, Rebecca McKillip, ill. II. Title.
  PR5489.L58 2011
  821'.8—dc22   2011004999

Printed in the United States of America in Mankato, Minnesota.
July 2011
PA02091

014-03769   Brad Beach   8/16/95   4-3

When at home alone I sit
and am very tired of it,

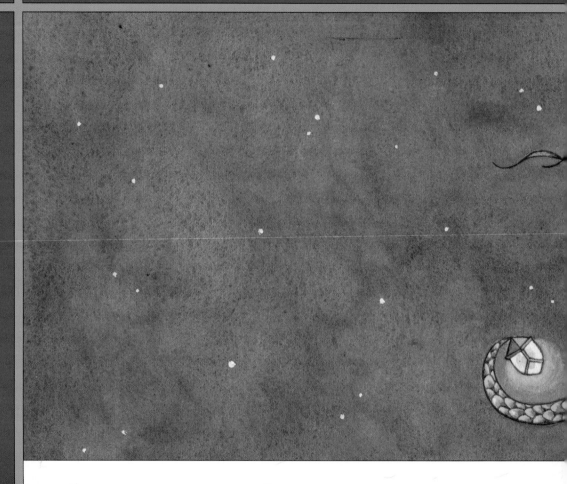

I have just to shut my eyes
to go sailing through the skies—

to go sailing far away . . .

to the pleasant Land of Play.

To the fairy land afar
where the Little People are;

Where the clover-tops are trees,

Harrison County
Public Library

and the rain-pools are the seas.

And the leaves like little ships . . .

sail about on tiny trips.

The Little Land

When at home alone I sit
And am very tired of it,
I have just to shut my eyes
To go sailing through the skies—
To go sailing far away
To the pleasant Land of Play.

To the fairy land afar
Where the Little People are;
Where the clover-tops are trees,
And the rain-pools are the seas,
And the leaves like little ships
Sail about on tiny trips.

—*Robert Louis Stevenson*

What makes a poem a poem?

With just a few words, a poem can make you feel things in a flash. It delights you, amazes you. It makes you laugh out loud or shed a tear. You know a poem is successful when it tickles your brain or touches your heart.

Poets choose their words very carefully. They don't just think about what words *mean*. They think about how they *sound*. Why write "sticky mess," when "mashed marshmallow" is so much more fun to say? Those repeating *m* sounds? They're alliteration in action!

Poets surprise you with similes and metaphors. A school hallway becomes a pirate's plank. A bed flies away in a dream. In this way, poets make their words come alive. A poem about a campfire makes you wrinkle your nose. A poem about a slithering snake makes you squirm in your seat.

Poets have all kinds of tools and tricks to make their work come alive. Maybe it's a rhyming verse. Maybe it's the rhythm of repeated sounds. Maybe it's the imagery of a melting ice cream cone. With the tricks of the trade, anything can become a poem!

About the Author

Robert Louis Stevenson was a famous writer and poet. He was born in Scotland in 1850. He was often sick as a child, and began to write stories to occupy his time. Stevenson is best known for writing the stories *Treasure Island*, *Kidnapped*, and *The Strange Case of Dr. Jekyll and Mr. Hyde*. Robert Louis Stevenson died in 1894.

About the Illustrator

Rebecca Thornburgh lives in a pleasantly spooky old house in Philadelphia. If she's not at her drawing table, she's reading— or singing with her band, called Reckless Amateurs. Rebecca has one husband, two daughters, and two silly dogs.

HARRISON COUNTY PUBLIC LIBRARY

3 MAIN 00167742 H